ELEPHANT QUEST

TED & BETSY LEWIN

HarperCollins*Publishers*

For Sheila, and all the wonderful staff at Xakánaxa Camp

Special thanks to James Doherty, Curator of Mammals,
Wildlife Conservation Society

Elephant Quest
Copyright © 2000 by Ted and Betsy Lewin
All rights reserved. Printed in Hong Kong
www.harperchildrens.com

Library of Congress Cataloging-in-Publication Data
Lewin, Ted.
Elephant quest / Ted & Betsy Lewin.
p.   cm.
Summary: Recounts an expedition through the Moremi Wildlife Reserve in Botswana,
describing the vegetation and wildlife, and culminating in the sighting of an African elephant herd.
ISBN 0-688-14111-0 (trade) — ISBN 0-688-14112-9 (library)
1. Zoology—Botswana—Moremi Wildlife Reserve   Juvenile literature.
2. African elephant—Moremi Wildlife Reserve—Juvenile literature.
[1. Moremi Wildlife Reserve (Botswana)   2. African elephant.   3. Elephants.]
I. Lewin, Betsy.   II. Title.
QL49.L387   2000   99-55369
591.96883—dc21

Design by Robbin Gourley
1 2 3 4 5 6 7 8 9 10
❖
First Edition

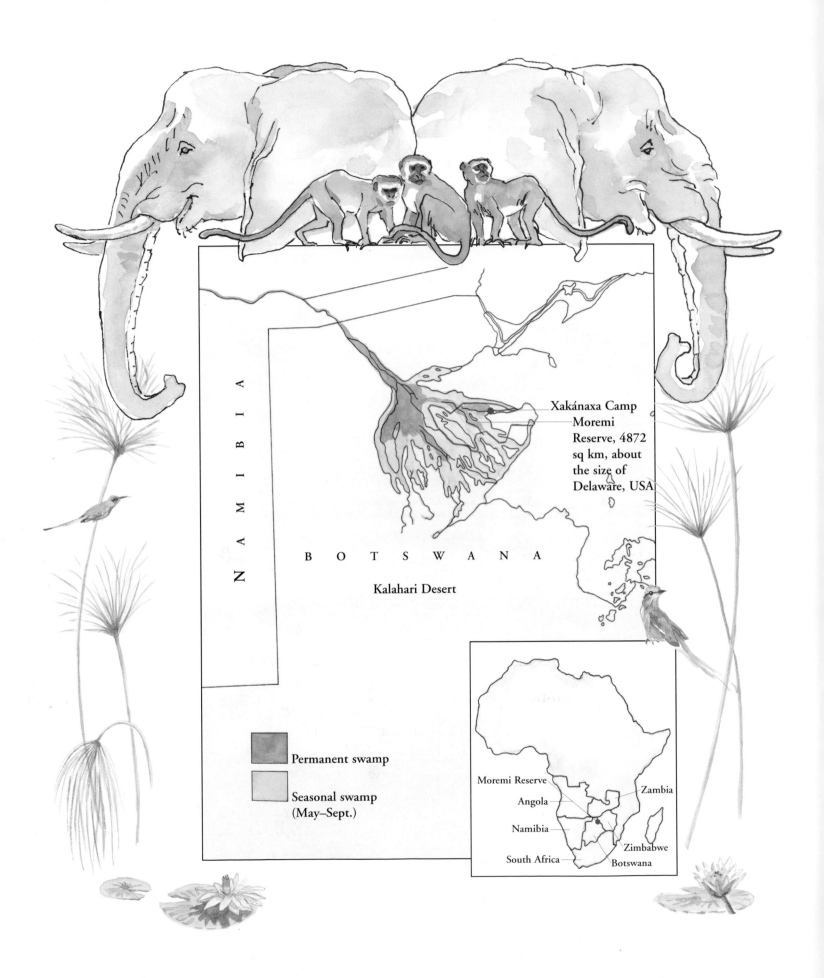

NAMIBIA

Xakánaxa Camp
Moremi
Reserve, 4872
sq km, about
the size of
Delaware, USA

B O T S W A N A

Kalahari Desert

Permanent swamp

Seasonal swamp
(May–Sept.)

Moremi Reserve
Angola
Namibia
South Africa

Zambia
Zimbabwe
Botswana

Early each year, in the highlands of Angola, the great Kavango River swells with rain. Months later, usually in May, its floodwaters begin to reach the Moremi Reserve in the Okavango Delta of Botswana. Rivers overflow, and water fills the open grasslands, saturates the ground, and flows on, finally exhausting itself in the Kalahari Desert.

By September, the flooded delta has begun to dry out. Then, in November or December, it starts to rain in the delta. The rains will last until March. Then in just a few months, the floods will arrive again from Angola.

Because there is always water in the delta, it is rich in animal life: hippos, buffalo, lions, leopards, wildebeest, lechwe, giraffes, and some seventy thousand elephants! It's the elephants we've especially come to see in this lush landscape.

We arrive in February—the rainy season in the Moremi Reserve. The rains have been heavy this year, and the ponds and flood plains are slowly filling with water, spilling over into one another, forming vast shallow lakes. Roads are disappearing under the lakes or becoming impassable because of mud.

Below us, the delta is a maze of islands, tall forests, papyrus-lined channels, deep lagoons, and secret pools. "Do you want me to fly lower?" Derek, our bush pilot, yells over the roar of the Cessna's engine. We nod, and the plane drops.

We can make out herds of wildebeest, zebras, and buffalo.
Giraffes cast long shadows on the plain. Suddenly we fly into
a thunderstorm. Derek banks the plane and drops down to
treetop level. He buzzes the landing strip, chasing off a herd of
impalas, then circles around and lands. Muddy water sprays
the windshield as we bump to a halt, and the motor sputters to
a stop.

At the edge of the forest, a young Bushman in a crisp khaki
uniform stands by a truck, waiting to take us to camp. He
smiles. "Welcome to Xakánaxa (ka-ká-na-ka)," he says. "I'm
Arabang, your driver."

Our camp is a dozen tents set up on wooden platforms

facing the Moanachira River, and in the middle of the river is the resident hippo. His

enormous mouth is wide open. We get the message loud and clear. This part of the river is his.

We unzip the mosquito net flap of our tent, step in, zip it back up, stow our gear, and

lie down on our beds. We're exhausted after our long journey. Lulled by the pattering rain,

we fall into a deep sleep.

DAY ONE—MORNING

The next morning the rain has stopped. The sun is just rising, and the night-foraging hippo is grazing his way down to the riverbank. As he passes, he flutters his tail and splatters our tent with dung. Then he pushes through the thick pampas grass at the edge of the river and settles in the water up to his ears. Day one of our elephant quest has begun.

There's just time for a quick cup of coffee before we climb into the back of a special Hilux truck that can plow through water like a hippo. Our morning game drive is under way. We'll come back to the camp around eleven, then go out again in the afternoon around three-thirty or four, returning at dusk. Mornings and late afternoons are the daylight hours when the animals are most active.

We pass under big jackalberry and sausage trees along the river and head for Dead Tree Island. It's not an island yet, but it soon will be. After last night's rain, the track outside the camp is underwater. Soon water will be everywhere.

Near a large mopane (mō-PAH-nē) tree not far from camp we find a huge fungus-termite mound, a twelve-foot-high sand-and-clay castle built by millions of termites, using their saliva as cement. Growing on the mound are enormous white mushrooms the size of pizzas. Their scientific name is *Termitomyces*, but the local people call them *mabua*. We climb down from the truck to pick them, stepping very carefully so as not to crush the new mushrooms just pushing up through the surface like white fists. Soon the back of the truck is filled with mushrooms. They are covered with beetles and other insects, but once they're washed clean, they will be wonderful to eat.

Dozens of vultures wheeling overhead lead us to a lion kill. There are three nearly grown cubs (about eighteen months old) lying by the track, licking the blood off one another's faces. Their mother and an older brother emerge from the tall grass and join in the grooming.

The kill is hidden in the grass. We can hear another lion crunching and cracking the bones.

Our driver tells us that this pride has recently been taken over by two strong young males, one of whom he calls Scarface. The feeding lion is Patches, one of the old deposed males. Patches' brother, Lazy Boy, hasn't been seen since the takeover.

The female leaves her cubs and joins Patches in the grass. A few minutes later Patches emerges, full-bellied, carrying the hind leg of a lechwe (a kind of antelope) in his mouth. He flops down in the shade of a shepherd's bush and gnaws on the leg halfheartedly. Vultures hunch in the trees all around, waiting for their turn at the kill.

Patches looks into the tall grass. He seems anxious.

Suddenly we hear a barked roar from the grass, and the female explodes onto the plain. Patches and the three cubs leap up and run for their lives.

A few minutes later we spot the female in a thicket, staring out across the plain. She snarls. One cub sits near her, gazing intently in the same direction, then bolts in terror.

Scarface bursts out of the grass, every ounce of his being bristling with murderous intent. He plunges into the thicket after the cub. He will not tolerate any cubs but his own, and he will kill the ones we have just been watching if he can catch them. But these cubs are nearly mature. If they can hide from Scarface for six more months, until they are two years old and able to outrun him, they will survive.

DAY ONE—AFTERNOON

There were no signs of elephants this morning, but we're hopeful about seeing them on our afternoon game drive. A short distance from camp, our driver stops and points into a deep thicket. We stare intently but see nothing except a tree stump and some twisted branches.

Suddenly the branches move and we realize that they are not branches at all but the spiral horns of a kudu bull. We can make out his white face markings now. Then more branches move, and we can see another pair of horns. If these animals hadn't moved, we would never have seen them at all.

Six feet at the shoulder, with horns like giant corkscrews, the kudu step elegantly from the thicket. A red-billed oxpecker rides on the back of one, picking off ticks. What a show! But it's not the one we're after. We're looking for elephants, but we're not destined to find them this afternoon.

That night, before we blow out the candles in our tent, we worry about the lion cubs and marvel at the two invisible seven-hundred-pound kudu. Could we have been looking right at elephants all day long and simply not seen them?

DAY TWO—MORNING

Despite our harvest, the termite mound is covered with mushrooms again this morning, but today a troop of chacma baboons has beaten us to them. They pull up the mushrooms, gorge on them, and also eat the termites as fast as they appear.

Not far away, we find a dead lion cub, a male, stinking in the hot sun—the work of Scarface. One of the cub's ears is gone, a bloody hole where it had been. Dozens of vultures wait in the dead trees, afraid to approach the carcass because the cub's mother might be nearby.

We are feeling sad at starting our day with this dead cub when suddenly a wild dog leaps out of the grass right in front of us. Then the rest of the pack appears, their round bat ears sticking straight up, their noses all pointed in the same direction, their white tails flashing. They trot across the road into the tall grass, twenty-seven in all. We see them leaping here, then there, above the grass as our truck bumps and lurches on the road alongside them. The pungent smell of wild sage fills the air as we scrape against it.

We turn a corner and all the dogs are right there, lying in the grass and on the road. We slam to a stop. They are alert, wild-eyed, and covered with blood from an earlier kill.

Suddenly they are up and running. We follow in the truck, almost part of the pack. They are coursing now—hunting on the run, by sight—only their black ears showing in the grass. They cross the road in front of us, working in relays.

They have an impala calf! The dogs form a circle around it, sink in their teeth, and tug in unison. In seconds, the calf is torn to shreds. The dogs come away with pieces.

They hardly pause to eat before they are off again, trotting onto an open grass plain. A herd of impalas feeds at the far end, completely unaware. The dogs spring from a trot to a flat-out run.

The impala herd bolts as one and heads for the mopane forest in great bounding leaps. The dogs follow. We see them in the forest, chasing the leaping impalas through the trees.

Our driver seems to know just where the dogs will come out, and we are there when they do. In the road in front of us, they stand on their hind legs or jump into the air to see over the tall marsh grass.

Then they plunge into the marsh.

19

The dogs flush a lechwe that bolts for safety into deeper water. Then the dogs appear in a channel, leaping and splashing through the water. One of them climbs a termite mound for a better view.

Back into the grass, the silent relentless hunt continues. We follow the dogs trotting steadily now, in a long line. They never seem to tire, and they never make a sound.

Finally, after an hour and a half, we lose them. We pass a herd of impalas, lying down and peaceful. The hunt is over, and the dogs have moved on.

DAY TWO—AFTERNOON

We pull out of camp after tea, passing an abandoned termite mound now occupied by a colony of dwarf mongooses. So tiny they could easily sit in the palm of your hand, the mongooses dart about. Constantly on the lookout for danger, their heads pop in and out of the termite-mound holes like little jack-in-the-boxes. Up ahead, a warthog sow "walks" on her horny knees, searching for roots and tubers in the sand. We startle her as we drive past, and she and her piglets are off and running, their tails sticking straight up. Farther along, a five-foot-long water monitor lizard waddles, his forked tongue flicking, from his burrow in the sand to a freshly flooded pond. But the afternoon brings no elephants.

Later we sit on the deck of our tent snacking on mopane worms, a delicacy enjoyed by the local people, who squeeze off the heads and fry the worms in hot oil. They are delicious, but the dim glow of our kerosene lantern makes them easier to swallow, since we can't really see what we're eating. It has been another extraordinary day, but where, we wonder, are the elephants? How can twelve-thousand-pound creatures be so hard to find?

DAY THREE—MORNING

We are awakened by the song of the Cape turtledove. It sounds like "Work HARDer, work HARDer, work HARDer." A gray lourie chimes in with a nasal "Go 'waaaaay, go 'waaaaay." We hope he's not calling to the elephants. As we get under way, a blacksmith plover leaps up from the roadside calling a metallic "Tink! Tink! Tink!"

A large herd of Cape buffalo materializes out of the mopane scrub, presenting a solid
bulwark of muscle and bone. They sniff the breeze for possible danger, but what could harm
them? Only elephants could make them move, and the elephants are nowhere to be seen.

The buffalo melt into the forest and we move on. Ahead, crossing the track right in front of us, the mother lion and her two remaining cubs head for the safety of the mopane scrub.

We come out onto a flooded grass plain where a herd of giraffes are feeding on candle-pod acacia. With their long black tongues and upper lips, they delicately pluck the tender leaves, which are surrounded by needle-sharp thorns. Sometimes, giraffes pick up pollen on their lips and noses and pollinate trees like bees. At nineteen feet, giraffes are the tallest animals on earth, and they are amazing.

One of them slowly, carefully spreads his front legs wide and lowers his head to drink. Even though they can weigh up to 2,600 pounds, in this position giraffes are vulnerable to lions, and this one is skittish as he drinks. Nearby, in a stand of acacia, a mother nurses her ten-foot-tall baby. Two young males spar playfully, swinging their heads at each other's bodies in an action called necking.

We follow our now-submerged track out onto the plain. At our approach, the giraffes break into their curious run. They move like rocking horses as they splash across the flooded plain, sending up sparkling sprays of water.

DAY THREE—AFTERNOON

This afternoon we pass the termite mound again, but today it is covered with birds instead of mushrooms. Glossy starlings, red- and yellow-billed hornbills, and helmeted shrikes all feast on termites crawling out of the mound to fly and mate.

At a place called Paradise Pools we spot a huge crocodile sunning himself on the far bank. He has swallowed an impala buck whole. Only its head and long curved horns protrude from the croc's mouth. As he lies there slowly digesting, he looks like a mythical monster.

In the muddy water ahead, a hammerkop shuffles its feet to scare up fish, worms, and frogs. The hammerkop (which means *hammerhead* in Afrikaans) gets its name from its large crest and bill. It nests in the forks of trees, in huge dome-shaped constructions of twigs and mud.

It is late in the day, and our hope of seeing elephants is sinking with the sun. Suddenly a large male leopard appears in the high grass in front of us. He climbs an old termite mound for a better view of the surrounding plain. The lowering sunlight strikes him on the shoulders as he gazes off in all directions. As he leaves the mound and walks into the setting sun, a full moon hangs in the bright sky behind him.

We return to camp and walk to our tent, shining flashlights into the trees, wary in the dark of the feeding hippo. He could be very dangerous if we got between him and the water.

DAY FOUR—MORNING

This morning we drive, hubcap-deep, onto a flooded grass plain. Our truck has special tires and can drive through the water with ease. The red lechwe have special hooves, so they also can run through the water with ease. When frightened, they head for deeper water, sometimes submerging with only their nostrils showing. In some places in the delta, lechwe herds cluster on floating islands of peat that wave underfoot as they feed.

The water keeps rising. More and more dry areas are now under water too deep to cross. A herd of wildebeest crosses a lush meadow, all spiky manes and unruly beards. They look like a combination of buffalo, antelope, and horse, all cobbled together.

We can go no farther—the water is too deep. We backtrack into the mopane scrub.

35

Suddenly, shrill trumpets sound behind every tree. We've found the elephants at last! In a pool deep in the mopane scrub, the giants of this garden squeal and splash and flap their ears, looking as joyful as we feel. In wallows nearby, some elephants are spraying muddy water all over themselves to protect their sensitive skins, and they glisten like wet bronze.

A group comes to the water's edge. Two tiny calves stand between their mothers and aunts and siphon water with their soft little trunks.

Our truck is downwind of them and they are unaware of us, but we keep the engine running just in case.

Some of the elephants are belly-deep in the water. Others lie on their sides, almost completely submerged, with only the tips of their trunks snorkeling the surface. Two mammoth mud wrestlers lock tusks and push and shove. They are quickly turning the pond into a big mud hole—and they seem to be having a very good time doing it.

Suddenly a huge female—the matriarch—steps out of the forest right behind us.

"Arabang!" we shout.

The elephant spreads her ears until she's as wide as the side of a barn and charges. Arabang jams down on the gas, and the wheels spin wildly. Finally they grab, and we lurch forward. The matriarch breaks off the charge and lumbers into the forest with a trumpeting scream and two short blasts.

We wanted to see elephants, but not *that* close!

The wind has shifted now, and one of the mud wrestlers sends her trunk up like a periscope. Trumpets blare. The wind has brought our scent, and with it, pandemonium. The giants splash off into the forest, the last one to leave shaking her head violently and slamming the water with her trunk before she too lumbers off.

The elephants will head for islands of high ground beyond our reach. Left behind on the soft clay banks are their huge footprints. When the ponds finally dry up, the empty footprints will remain in the sun-baked clay until they're filled again by the rains here in the delta.

The next day, we are on our way home. We say good-bye to the resident hippo, then pack up our gear, put it in the back of the Hilux, and head for the airstrip. We can hear the Cessna coming in for a landing long before we get there.

Derek helps us stow our gear as we regale him with stories of our elephant quest. Then we buckle up and he taxis to the end of the strip, turns into the wind, and we roar into the sky. As our Cessna gains altitude, we look back down over the delta.

It surprises us to see that it's practically empty. No herds of wildebeest or giraffes or buffalo, or even lechwe. We spot only one kind of animal on the great plain below—a huge herd of elephants right out in the open for all the world to see. Looking down on this, who would believe we had such trouble finding them?

Smiling, we settle back into our seats and close our eyes.

African Elephant Facts

Common name: African elephant
Male: bull
Female: cow
Baby: calf

Scientific name: Loxodonta africana

Weight: Up to 13,000 pounds—the largest land mammal. An elephant's tail alone can weigh up to 22 pounds.

Height: Up to 13 feet at the shoulder

Diet: Twigs and bark of trees, grass, leaves, roots, fruits. Adult African elephants may consume 400 pounds or more of food each day.

Gestation period: 22 months. At birth, a calf weighs 200 to 300 pounds and stands nearly 3 feet high at the shoulder.

Estimated life span: 60 to 70 years

Predators: Man. Calves may be attacked by lions and hyenas.

Conservation status: Threatened by poaching for meat and ivory. Elephants also face habitat loss due to expanding human populations.

TRUNK

An adult African elephant's trunk is an extension of its nose and upper lip. It has 150,000 muscles and is strong enough to kill an animal as large as a buffalo with one blow. Two "fingers" at the tip of the trunk enable it to pick up an object as small as a dime. A trunk can weigh up to 350 pounds; elephants often drape their trunks over their tusks to lighten the load.

Elephants use their trunks to gather food, and they drink by sucking water up through their trunks, then squirting it into their mouths. They also use their trunks for smelling and fighting and for spraying mud over their backs to protect their sensitive skin from sun and parasites. An elephant may place its trunk into another's mouth as a gesture of reassurance.

TUSKS

Both males and females have tusks. The longest ever measured was 11 feet, 1¼ inches. The heaviest measured weighed 226 pounds. Elephants are usually right- or left-"handed," using one tusk more than the other. Over time, the favored tusk becomes worn or even broken off. Elephants use their tusks to lift things, to search for food by digging up roots and prying off tree bark, and as weapons when fighting.

TEETH

An elephant's molars, which are used for grinding food, can be replaced up to six times in a lifetime. When its last pair of molars wears down, the elephant can no longer easily feed and is near the end of its life.

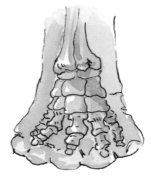

EARS

An African elephant's ears are huge, about 110 pounds each. An elephant fans them back and forth to cool off and spreads them as a threat or when it intends to charge.

FEET

Feet are covered with thick pads, enabling elephants to walk very quietly. They walk on tiptoe and can run for short distances at a speed of 25 miles per hour.

PLAY

Elephants love to play. The young have mock battles, wrestle, and play tag. They seem to enjoy splashing in water as much as human children do. We once watched a baby elephant play-charge at us, trumpeting, kicking up dust, and turning in circles, then collapsing on its side to blow puffs of dust up with its trunk. Elephants are also intensely curious. We once saw an elephant and her calf in Uganda watching an outdoor Elvis Presley movie, in which they seemed to take great pleasure.

FAMILY LIFE

African elephants are social and gregarious. Mothers, aunts, and elder siblings all help in raising and protecting the young. Adults teach calves what to eat. Elephants have been observed helping sick or injured family members by shading them, giving them water, attempting to help them to their feet, and leading them away from danger. They have even been observed helping members of other species out of trouble.

Some researchers believe that elephants have a concept of death. They've been observed examining, smelling, picking up, and carrying the bones of their dead, especially skulls and tusks. They've also been known to cover their dead with leaves and branches.

COMMUNICATION

African elephants make many sounds. They trumpet, grunt, rumble, squeal, and even purr, seeming to have different sounds for different emotions. They can communicate over very long distances with low-frequency sounds inaudible to the human ear, and have been known to react to distress signals from another herd nearly 100 miles away.

INDEX

Illustrations shown by *italics*

Acacia. *See* Candle-pod acacia
African elephants (*Loxodonta africana*),
    5, *36–39*, 47
    charge by matriarch, 40, *40–41*
    communication, 47
    diet, 46
    difficulty finding, 16, 23, 33, 45
    ears, 47
    family life, 47
    feet, 47, *47*
    flight by, 42–43, *42–43*
    footprints, 43
    life span, 46
    playfulness, 36, 39, 47
    predators, 46
    pregnancy, 46
    skin, 36
    teeth, 47, *47*
    trunk, 46, *46*
    tusks, *46*, 46–47
    weight, 46
Air, views from, *6*, 6–7, *44–45*, *44–45*
Antelope. *See* Lechwe
Arabang (driver), *7*, 13, 16, 40

Baboons. *See* Chacma baboons
Blacksmith plover, 24
Botswana, map of, *4*
Buffalo. *See* Cape buffalo

Candle-pod acacia, 26, 27
Cape buffalo, 5, *24–25*, 25–26
Cape turtledove, 24
Chacma baboons, 18, *18*
Crocodile, 30, *30*

Elephants. *See* African elephants

Giraffes, 5, 26–27, *26–29*
Gray lourie, 24

Hammerkop (hammerhead bird), 30, *31*
Hilux truck, *7*, *10*, 11, 35, *35*, *40*
Hippopotamus, 5, 8, *8–9*, 11, 33
Hornbills, 30

Impalas, 7, *7*
    as crocodile food, 30
    hunting of, 19–21
Jackalberry trees, 11

Kalahari Desert, *4*, 5
Kavango River, 5
Kudu, 16, *16–17*

Lechwe (antelope), 5, 13, *34–35*, 35
    hunting of, 20
Leopards, *32–33*, 33
Lions, 5, *12–15*, 18
    attacks on elephant calves, 46
    dangers faced by cubs, 13–14, 18,
        26, *26*
    eating/social behavior, 12–14

Mabua mushrooms, 12, *12*, 18, *18*
Map, *4*
Moanachira River, 8
Mongooses, 23, *23*
Mopane scrub, 12
    discovery of elephants in, 36
    protection offered by, 26
Mopane worms, eating of, 23, *23*
Moremi Reserve, *4*, 5–6
Mushrooms (*Termitomyces*), 12, *12*, 18,
    18

Night-foraging, 11

Okavango Delta (Botswana)
    abundance of life in, 5
    emptiness of, 44–45
    rainy season, 6, *6*, 11, 35
    seasonal changes, 5, 43
    views from above, *6*, 44–45, *44–45*

Patches (lion), 13

Rainy season, 5–6, 11, 35
Red-billed oxpecker, 16, *17*

Sausage trees, 11
Scarface (lion), 13–14, *14–15*
Shrikes, 30
Starlings, 30

Termite mounds
    baboons on, 18, *18*
    birds on, 30, *30*
    mongooses on, 23, *23*
    mushrooms on, 12, *12*, 18, *18*
Termitomyces (*mabua*) mushrooms, 12,
    12, 18, *18*

Vultures, 12–13, 18

Warthogs, 23, *23*
Water monitor lizard, *22*, 23
Wild dogs, 18, *18–19*
    impala hunting, 19–21, *20–21*
Wildebeest, 5, 35, *35*

Xakánaxa, 7–8